Tickles, Pickles, and Floofing Persnickles

Reading and Writing Nonsense Poems

compiled and annotated by Jill Kalz

PICTURE WINDOW BOOKS
a capstone imprint

Special thanks to our adviser for his expertise:

Terry Flaherty, PhD, Professor of English
Minnesota State University, Mankato

Editor: Jill Kalz
Designer: Lori Bye
Art Director: Nathan Gassman
Production Specialist: Kathy McColley

Illustration Credits
Cristian Bernardini, 4, 5, 9, 22, 28, 29, 32; Dustin Burkes-Larrañaga, 1, 8, 12-13, 24, 26-27; Sandra D'Antonio, 7, 20, 21, 23, 31; Matt Loveridge, cover, back cover, 2-3, 6, 11, 14, 17, 25; Simon Smith, 18; Tou Yia Xiong, 10, 15, 16, 19

Picture Window Books are published by Capstone,
1710 Roe Crest Drive, North Mankato, Minnesota 56003
www.capstonepub.com

Library of Congress Cataloging-in-Publication Data
Cataloging-in-publication information is on file with the Library of Congress.
ISBN 978-1-4795-2198-2 (library binding)
ISBN 978-1-4795-2949-0 (paperback)
ISBN 978-1-4795-3332-9 (eBook PDF)

Printed in the United States of America in Brainerd, Minnesota.
092013 007770BANGS14

TABLE OF CONTENTS

DISCOVER THE POET IN YOU

Poetry doesn't have to be serious. Really! It can be funny. Goofy. Zany. Weird. It can include made-up words and creatures. It can be about disgusting stuff. Poetry allows you to play with language and word sounds, subjects and forms. No two people see the world exactly the same way. Share all the silly nonsense swimming in your imagination by writing a poem.

WHY WRITE POETRY?

When you write poetry, you're an explorer. You discover new words, new combinations of words, and new meanings. You use old words in fresh ways. Poetry opens your ears. Sentences can play like music. Poetry opens your eyes. It's as if you're seeing the world around you—your ordinary, everyday world—for the very first time. Poetry can be a new language that allows you to share your ideas and experiences.

WHAT TOOLS DOES A POET USE?

Whether you're building a house, a car, or a video game, you need tools to get the job done. Poets use tools to build their poems too. Their tools include parts of speech (such as nouns, verbs, and adjectives), ways of writing (like different forms or types of poetry), and the cool sounds that letters and words make when they're combined (like rhymes and repeated letters). Knowing what the tools are and how to use them is what this book is all about.

HOW DO I READ THIS BOOK?

Start by reading the poems. All of them are about silly things. After you read each one, take a look at the Info Box on the bottom of the page. There you'll find definitions of poetic forms and tools. You may also find helpful tips, questions to consider, or writing prompts. Near the back of the book, you'll have the chance to review what you've learned and practice writing your own poems. Before you know it, you'll be a poet!

The Girl Who Loved Beans

There once was a girl who loved beans.
She ate them by most any means.
So many she ate
that it was her fate
to toot holes in her brand-new blue jeans.

—Connie Colwell Miller

SOUNDS LIKE ...

When words end in the same sound, they **rhyme**. In the poem above, "beans," "means," and "jeans" rhyme. So do "ate" and "fate." Rhyming words can add interest and structure to a poem. Try making a list of words that rhyme with "girl."

What My Dad's Cooking

dinner
brown, meaty
sizzling, snapping, splattering
pepper, onions, leather, oil
smoking, spitting, burning
slimy, tough
liver

—Blake Hoena

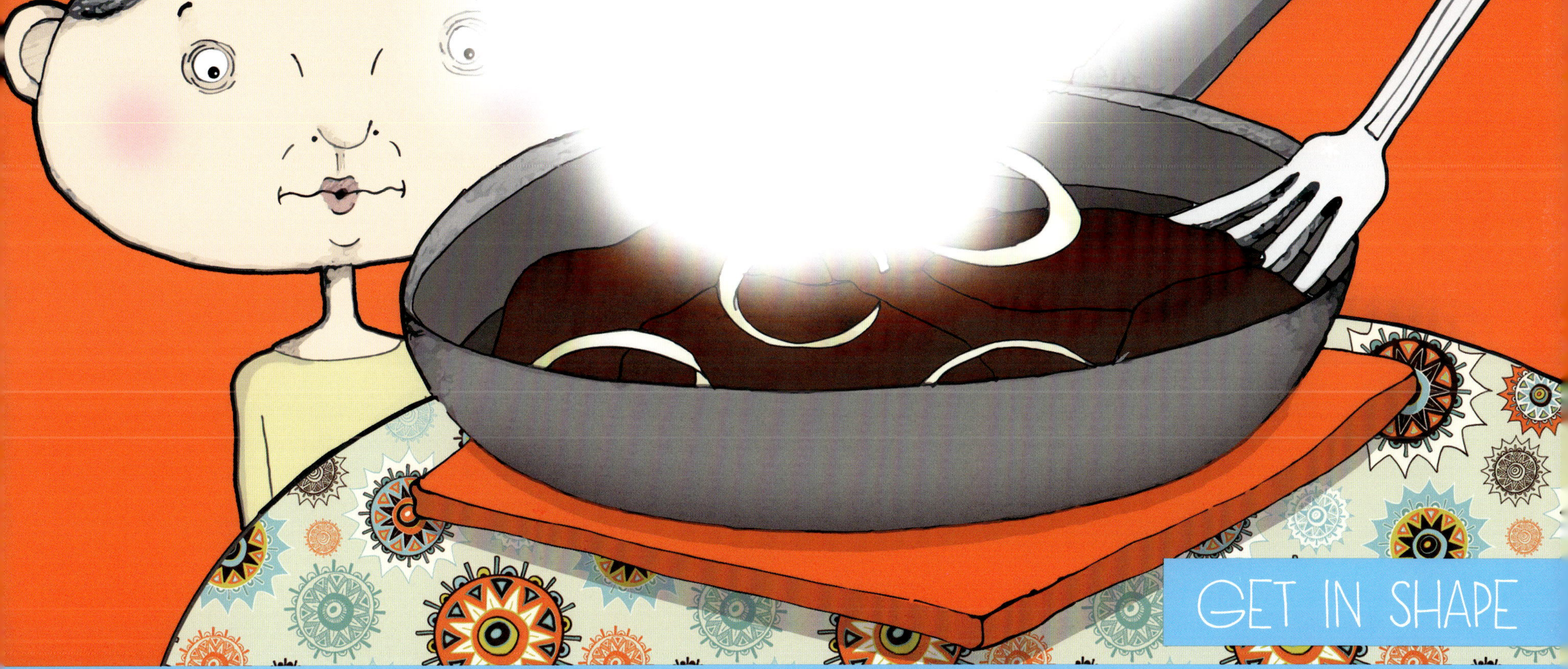

GET IN SHAPE

The diamond-shaped **diamante** uses a parts-of-speech pattern. The seven-line poem starts with a noun. Two adjectives and three verbs follow. Next come four nouns, three verbs, and two adjectives. The final noun is often the opposite of the first.

The Man in the Moon

Whoa,
look up there!
The man in the moon! Do
you hear his tempting tune? His lips
are round, his eyes shut tight. His glow
invites you into the night. Will you come
play? Hey, where's his nose? The stars around
him dance on toes. And out you go, despite
your fright. You frolic and howl throughout
the night. See, the boogeyman can't stand
a chance when the man in the moon
invites you to dance. So when you
see his singing lips, open your
window! Wiggle those
hips!

—Catherine Ipcizade

PICTURE POEM

Concrete poems look like their subjects. See how the poem above talks about the moon and looks like the moon too?

You could also use this shape to write a poem about a basketball, an orange, or a penny. What other subjects would work?

Tall and Short

Too-Tall Tom and So-Short Sal
lived together near the sea.
The wonderful things that Tom could reach
Sal just couldn't see.

Just as bad, you might have guessed,
were those treasures on the ground
that So-Short Sal could grab with ease
but proved too small for Tom.

So Too-Tall Tom brought his things down
and showed them to So-Short Sal.
And So-Short Sal tossed his things up
to share them all with Tom.

—Connie Colwell Miller

STICKING TOGETHER

A **stanza** is a group of lines that is usually separated by a blank line, called a **stanza break**. Stanzas often contain complete thoughts. Here the first stanza is about Tom's abilities, the second is about Sal's, and the third is about the pair working together.

The Tiki Man

"Do not take the tiki man.
He lives within the island sand."
And yet I took him for my loot.
He was so little and so cute!
But they had warned me, yes, they had:
"To take an island trinket's bad!"
I brought him home,
and luck went sour.
Something every single hour!
My hair was tangled,
my bicycle mangled,
my homework fell in a hole.
I ate the cat's kibble.
My milk, it dribbled.
I ran into a pole!
And so I hopped right on a plane.
That tiki went away.
I placed him deep into the sand,
and left him there to stay!

—Catherine Ipcizade

TELL ME A STORY

Narrative poems tell stories. Other than that, there aren't any rules. They may be long or short, rhyming or not. The stories may be simple or complex. They may include action and **dialogue**. What details does this poet use to keep you interested in the story?

No Need to Shower When Your Pet's a St. Bernard

He shakes
his massive head,
and gobs of slobber fly,
showering the walls, the TV,
and me.

—Blake Hoena

FIVE LINES

A **cinquain** (sin-CANE) is a five-line poem. "Cinq" means "five" in French. The poem follows a 2-4-6-8-2 pattern of **syllables**.

Count the syllables in the poem above with your fingers. Feel the pattern? Now write a cinquain about a talkative parrot.

The Bedbug

There's a bedbug on my pillow
And I think he plans to stay.
Each time I put my head down
He insists I go away.
"What right," he says, "do you have
To lay your greasy hair
Upon my humble home, sir?
Please take a little care!"

"No bedbug gets the best of me!"
I cry out as I swat.
Just when I think I've got him
I discover I have not.
He's sprung up off the bedding
And landed on my nose.
Before I know what hits me,
His fists rain savage blows.

CAN YOU FEEL IT?

Rhythm is the "drum" in poetry. It can be created by **beats** or syllables. You can measure rhythm in **meter**—just count the beats or stressed syllables in each line. Read aloud, and tap the beats with your finger: "There's a BED-bug ON my PIL-low ..."

His right-hook is a mean one.
His left-jab smarts a lot.
My schnoz becomes a punching bag.
He gives it all he's got!
The room begins to tip and spin.
My eyes have filled with tears.
I crash headlong upon the bed.
His wee-voice fills my ears:

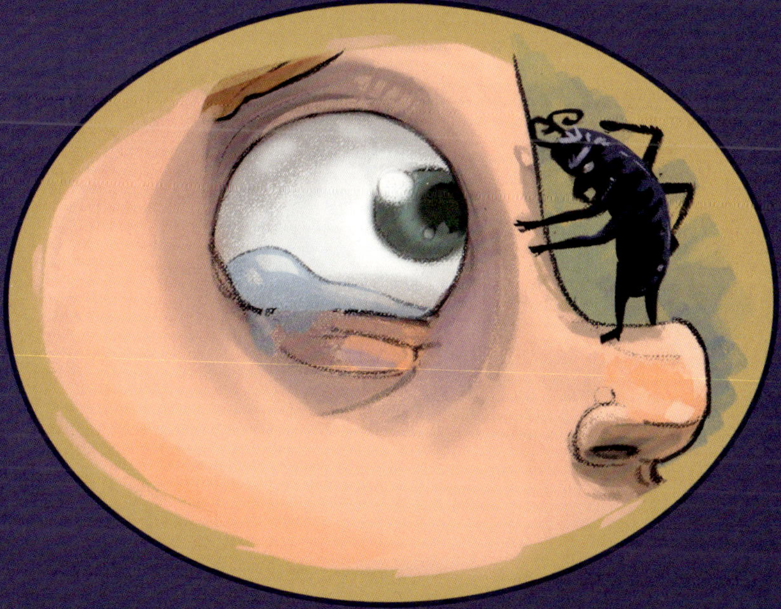

"Take a kindly tip from me,
You low-down, ugly mug.
Never pick a fistfight
With a bedbug that can slug."

—Christopher L. Harbo

Summer

Splickity splash! Water baths!
Under backyard forts we dash!
Muddy legs and sweaty grins,
Melon dripping down our chins.
Everyone plays ding-dong-ditch.
Run! Run! RUN! Don't you snitch!

—Catherine Ipcizade

HIDE AND SEEK

An **acrostic** is a poem with a secret. When the first letter of each line is put together, it spells another word or phrase. Sometimes that hidden message is the poem's main idea or title of the poem. Try writing an acrostic about your favorite holiday.

Why Mom Hates Doing My Laundry

Gooey bubble gum
tugs at the soles of my shoes.
I'm wearing white socks.

—Blake Hoena

WHAT'S NEW, HAIKU?

A **haiku** is a Japanese form of poetry. It has three lines and follows a 5-7-5 pattern of syllables. Lines 1 and 3 have five syllables. Line 2 has seven. Why does Mom hate doing the speaker's laundry? The poem tells why. Why is it important that the socks are white?

What's That Smell Following Me?

What's that smell following me?
It's kind of yellow and somewhat green,
with bright orange stripes
swirling around wherever I go.

What's that smell following me?
It's churning and gurgling,
with huge bursting bubbles
that splatter about wherever I go.

What's that smell following me?
It's like rotten eggs, moldy cheese,
dirty diapers, and stinky socks
littering the ground wherever I go.

What's that smell following me?
It has burly arms and fingers of steel
that spin me around till I'm dizzy
and stumble about wherever I go.

What's that smell following me?
I can almost taste it slithering
like worms and grubs squirming
across my tongue wherever I go.

What's that smell following me?
Oh wait, it's my tennis shoes!

—Blake Hoena

AGAIN AND AGAIN

When poets use **repetition**, they repeat certain words, phrases, or sounds. Every stanza in this poem begins with the same phrase. And nearly all of the stanzas end with "wherever I go." Repetition helps create patterns that hold the poem together.

Floofing Persnickles

You hear the propellers, roll
your eyes toward the sky, expecting
a high-flying plane, clouds,
a bird or two, but there,
falling fast through the blue,
is a pair of persnickles—
grinning, goggled persnickles,
floofing with parachutes!

"Yoo-hoo!" you shout to the
skydiving beasts. "I once saw you
flurfing, another time blurfing.
I even saw a herd of you slurfing.
But floofing is new, and I'm
tickled to see it! Could you lend
me a chute, teach me to floof?
I promise to learn quick and listen."

But those snickering persnickles just floated away
with a wave and wink, tails steering like rudders.

—Clara Cella

THE RHYME INSIDE

Not all rhymes happen at the ends of poetry lines. Sometimes they happen within lines. **Internal rhymes** create a fun echo of sound. Hear the "sky / flying" and "two / blue" rhymes in the first stanza of this poem? What other rhymes can you find?

Bugs!

If flies are bugs that fly and buzz,
then what do bumblebees do?
They fly, too, and buzz as well,
and they also rather bug me.
I really can't say what bugs me worse—
a buzzing fly or a flying bee
or a simply buggy beetle.

—Connie Colwell Miller

ITS OWN WAY

A **free verse** poem finds its own shape. It doesn't follow a fixed rhythm or meter. Repeating words or sounds may help hold the poem together. In this poem, the word "fly" repeats a lot. What other words repeat? What effect do these repeated words have?

Riding My Rhino to the Store

Did you know that once I rode my rhino to the store?
It was a day, a summer day, and the world seemed quite a bore.

So I went out back and unlatched the fence and nudged my rhino out.
I poked his butt and honked his horn and then I gave a shout.

He looked at me and rolled his eyes and said, "OK. Let's go."
And off we went down Main Street, giving quite a show.

We walked until we'd reached the place where all the treats were sold.
We bought some candy, ate it up, and returned home good as gold.

That was the day I rode my rhino all the way downtown.
I'll do it again, same as before, next time I'm feeling down.

—Connie Colwell Miller

QUITE A PAIR

A pair of poetry lines is called a **couplet**. The lines usually rhyme, as in this poem. A couplet often stands as a unit, making its own image or point. Try writing a rhyming couplet about a sneezing chipmunk in need of a tissue.

Spork

I'm neither a spoon nor a fork.
I'm handy for cream sauce or pork.
I'll scoop up your soup
Or spear beans by the group.
Such is the life of a spork.

—Christopher L. Harbo

SOMETHING SILLY

A **limerick** is a fun five-line poem. The first, second, and last lines rhyme ("fork / pork / spork"). The third and fourth lines are shorter and rhyme with each other ("soup / group"). Try writing a limerick about waffles or a talking horse.

Sounds My Body Makes

1
My tummy is burbling
and gurgling,
grumbling and rumbling too.
I'll need to run and find the bathroom soon.

2
Poor me, I'm wheezing
and sneezing,
honking and blowing my nose.
This is getting to be a pretty nasty cold.

3
And now, I'm choking
and croaking,
gagging and hurling green gunk.
Aunt Sally made mystery casserole for lunch.

4
I can't stop burping
and belching,
hiccupping toxic gas.
I gulped down my orange soda a bit too fast.

5
Finally I am snorting
and snuffling,
and snoring loud as a pirate.
Even in sleep, my body can't keep quiet.

—Blake Hoena

PERFECT PICTURES

Imagery is what you picture in your mind when you read a poem. Details like colors, sounds, textures, smells, and flavors all help create imagery. In this poem, the poet uses strong verbs such as "gurgling" and "snuffling" to help us "see" the sounds.

The Things That Haunt My Closet

Aren't hairy monsters or creepy ghosts.
What makes me quiver under the blankets
At night, what really scares me the most,
Are all the things I stuffed in my closet

And then completely forgot about,
Like an empty jar of peanut butter,
The newspapers from my paper route,
And some broccoli from last night's supper.

There's a hornet's nest and my trombone,
Stacks of comic books and dirty clothes,
A tube of toothpaste and the volcano
From science class that wouldn't explode.

There are baseballs and stinky shoes.
Collections of rocks, bugs, and keys,
Along with my pet mice, Benny and June,
So I made sure to throw in some string cheese.

One day, my mother wanted to clean
My closet out; I still hear her in there,
But it's been weeks since she was last seen.
I just hope she hasn't found my pet bear.

—Blake Hoena

COUNT TO FOUR

A stanza with four lines is called a **quatrain**. The poem above is made of rhyming quatrains that follow an ABAB pattern. The ends of the first and third lines rhyme ("ghosts / most"). So do the second and fourth lines ("blankets / closet").

Ode to My Toilet

I named it John,
the can in my bathroom,
the one that I sit on
when I go Number Two.
It's my Grecian urn,
my porcelain throne.
When my tummy churns,
please leave us alone.

I'll sit there for hours
on my bleached white loo.
It won't smell like flowers,
doing what I have to do.
But with one simple flush,
John will be ready again,
even if Dad made lunch—
fried liver and onions.

My lavatory, my commode,
My latrine to whiz in ...
You're a perfect home
for my round rear end.

—Blake Hoena

An **ode** is a type of **lyric poem**. It's usually written in three stanzas of varying line length. Like all lyric poems, odes are personal and full of strong feelings. The poem above is certainly personal! About what (or whom) would you like to write an ode?

Spot the Dog

The sky was blue; the sun was hot
the day I learned my dog could talk.
Such a good dog, my brown dog Spot.
We were taking our daily walk.
Suddenly, Spot cleared his throat,
looked up at me and smartly spoke,
"My boy, it really gets my goat
that you call me Spot. Is it some joke?"
My eyes got wide; my mouth dropped open.
I couldn't believe what I had heard.
My dog named Spot had not only spoken
but perfectly pronounced each single word.
So on that day I changed his name 'round.
From that day forward, Spot's name was Brown.

—Connie Colwell Miller

SEE A PATTERN?

A poem can feel more complete when it follows a rhyming pattern, like this **sonnet**. The pattern here is ABABCDCDEFEFGG.

The ends of lines 1 and 3 rhyme ("A"). So do lines 2 and 4 ("B"). Which words in the poem do "C," "D," "E," "F," and "G" represent?

Smooooth Sailing

I walked into the barn,
and the cow said to me,
"I'd really like to leave this farm
and see what I can see.
Seagulls say the beach is nice,
cool waves and golden sand.
But eagles say a mountain peak
is a lovely place to land."

I told the cow I'd try my best
to moooove her off the farm,
but the chickens heard our little plan
and sounded the alarm.
"Cluck! Cluck! Squawk! Squawk!
The cow is on the run.
Packed her bags and headed east
in search of seaside fun!"

—Clara Cella

TO BE HUMAN

When poets use **personification**, they make non-human things seem human. Real birds and cows don't talk like people. But in the poem above, they do. This fun-seeking cow even owns a couple suitcases! See if you can personify a bicycle or an earthworm.

The Monster Who Was Afraid of Loud Noises

Frank was scary to look at, with his large, toothy fangs.
He liked to smile at children—so in fear they would shake!
But when they cried, Frank cried too, and ran away afraid.

Now what was a scary monster like Frank supposed to do
If his job was making people jump right out of their shoes?
Late one night he scared a boy by loudly shouting, *BOO!*

The boy screamed, and toothy Frank nearly had a heart attack.
Are you afraid you scared me? the boy just had to ask.
I don't like loud noises, Frank the monster whispered back.

TELLING TALES

A **ballad** tells a story, usually about a hero or a memorable event. It often contains action, dialogue, and a rhyming pattern.

Long ago, ballads weren't written down. They were shared by word of mouth. As a result, ballads often changed over time.

Hmmm, the boy thought about that, what he had been told.
I know a lot about monsters, because I'm just ten years old.
They all are afraid of something. Bet you didn't know,

Drac bites with eyes closed, the sight of blood makes him faint,
Millie the Ghost stays in her house, so I guess she's afraid
Of being outside, and Wolfy, he fears flowering wolfsbane.

Lastly the boy asked, *Why can't you just cover your ears*
when you scare someone? Then their screams you wouldn't hear.
Doing just that, Frank yelled, *Boo!* And the boy ran away in fear.

—Blake Hoena

PRACTICE IT!

Starting to understand the tools poets use? There are lots of them! The following questions will help you practice with a few tools first before you sit down to write. (Hint: Find a word you don't understand? Look in the Glossary on page 30.)

- When words end in the same sound, they rhyme, such as in the poem "Riding My Rhino to the Store" on page 19. Find other poems in this book that have rhyming lines. Do the rhymes always appear in a pattern?

- **Alliteration** is a tool that creates interest in a poem. It repeats leading consonant sounds that are the same. Look at "What's That Smell Following Me?" (page 16). The words "bursting bubbles," "dirty diapers," and "smelly socks" are examples of alliteration. Find at least three other poems that use alliteration.

- In "Tall and Short" (page 9), the poet separates groups of lines and ideas with stanzas. Find other poems that use stanzas.

- "Bugs!" (page 18) is a free verse poem—it doesn't use a pattern of rhyming words or rhythms. Find another example of free verse in this book.

- You can get a good picture of a poem because of imagery. Which poems created good pictures in your mind? What were some of the details in those poems?

- You read in "Floofing Persnickles" (page 17) that the persnickles used their tails "like rudders" because of **similes**. Similes make comparisons by saying one thing is *like* another. **Metaphors**, on the other hand, make comparisons without the use of the words "like" or "as." Find another poem that uses a simile to help describe something.

WRITE IT!

Here's an activity that will help you discover the poet in you!

GET TO KNOW A FLOOFING PERSNICKLE

One of the best things about writing nonsense poems is that you can be as goofy as you want to be. You can make up words, names, creatures, places ... Think about Dr. Seuss. He let his imagination take him everywhere! He created Truffula Trees, creatures called Sneetches, and the Whos of Who-ville.

1) REREAD THE POEM "FLOOFING PERSNICKLES" ON PAGE 17.

Take some time to get a good picture in your mind of what persnickles look, act, and sound like. If "floofing" involves a parachute, what do you think "flurfing" and "blurfing" are?

2) GET A PEN AND A NOTEBOOK.

3) TRY WRITING AN ACROSTIC ABOUT THESE CREATURES.

The first letter of each line should spell out the word "persnickle." If you need help, use the poem "Summer" (page 14) as an example.

4) NOW MAKE UP YOUR OWN SPECIAL CREATURE WITH ITS OWN SPECIAL NAME.

Try writing a limerick about it. You might begin, "I once saw a blubbering balloo / eat a whole peach pie, then two ..." Use "Spork" (page 20) as an example.

GLOSSARY

acrostic—a poem that uses the first letters of each line to spell out a word, name, or phrase relating to the poem's topic

alliteration—the use of two or more words that start with the same letter sound

ballad—a rhythmic poem that tells a story and is often sung

beat—a stressed word or syllable in a line of poetry

cinquain—a five-line poem that follows a 2-4-6-8-2 pattern of syllables

concrete poem—a poem that takes the shape of its subject

couplet—a pair of rhyming lines that usually have the same number of beats; couplets make their own point, create a separate image, or summarize the idea of a poem

dialogue—the words spoken between two or more characters (people or creatures); in writing, dialogue is set off with quotation marks

diamante—a seven-line poem that forms a diamond shape and follows this pattern: 1 noun, 2 adjectives, 3 verbs, 4 nouns, 3 verbs, 2 adjectives, 1 noun

free verse—a poem that follows no set rhythm or meter

haiku—a three-line poem that follows a 5-7-5 pattern of syllables

imagery—language that creates pictures in a reader's mind

internal rhyme—a word within a line of poetry that sounds like another word either at the end of the same line or within another line

limerick—a silly five-line poem in which the first two lines rhyme with the last, and the third and fourth lines rhyme with each other

lyric poem—a poem that expresses strong, personal feelings; sonnets, odes, and elegies are examples of lyric poetry

metaphor—a figure of speech that compares different things without using words such as "like" or "as"

meter—the pattern of beats in each line of a poem

narrative poem—a poem that tells a story

ode—a type of lyric poem, usually written in three stanzas with varying line lengths

personification—giving human characteristics, or traits, to something that isn't human

quatrain—a four-line group of poetry

repetition—saying something again and again

rhyme—word endings that sound the same

rhythm—a pattern of beats, like in music

simile—a figure of speech that compares different things by using the words "like" or "as"

sonnet—a poem that has 14 lines and a fixed pattern of rhymes

stanza—a grouping of lines in poetry

stanza break—the blank line that separates stanzas

syllable—a unit of sound in a word

READ MORE

Fandel, Jennifer. *You Can Write Cool Poems.* You Can Write. North Mankato, Minn.: Capstone Press, 2012.

Lear, Edward, and masterminded by Daniel Pinkwater. *His Shoes Were Far Too Tight.* San Francisco: Chronicle Books, 2011.

Prelutsky, Jack, poems selected by. *Read a Rhyme, Write a Rhyme.* New York: Alfred A. Knopf, 2005.

Salas, Laura Purdie. *Picture Yourself Writing Poetry: Using Photos to Inspire Writing.* See It, Write It. Mankato, Minn.: Capstone Press, 2012.

Silverstein, Shel. *Every Thing on It: Poems and Drawings.* New York: Harper, 2011.

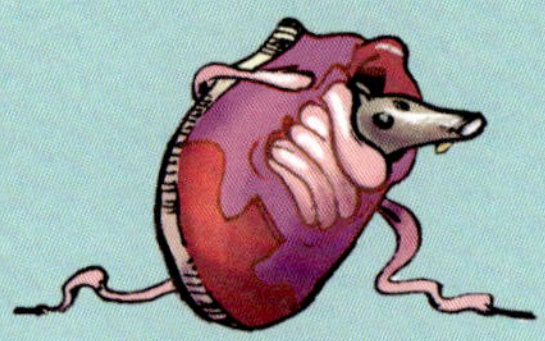

LOOK FOR ALL THE BOOKS IN THE SERIES:

PUCKS, CLUBS, AND BASEBALL GLOVES: READING AND WRITING SPORTS POEMS

THORNS, HORNS, AND CRESCENT MOONS: READING AND WRITING NATURE POEMS

TICKLES, PICKLES, AND FLOOFING PERSNICKLES: READING AND WRITING NONSENSE POEMS

TRUST, TRUTH, AND RIDICULOUS GOOFS: READING AND WRITING FRIENDSHIP POEMS

INTERNET SITES

FactHound offers a safe, fun way to find Internet sites related to this book. All of the sites on FactHound have been researched by our staff.

Here's all you do:
Visit *www.facthound.com*
Type in this code: 9781479521982